POEMS AND SONGS

POEMS & SONGS
By RICHARD MIDDLETON

With an Introduction
by Henry Savage

WILDSIDE PRESS

Published by
Wildside Press, LLC
P.O. Box 301
Holicong, PA 18928-0301 USA
www.wildsidepress.com

Wildside Press Edition: MMIII

TO

FRANK HARRIS

SHAKESPEARE'S INTIMATE, THE CREATOR OF

ELDER CONKLIN, MONTES AND THE BOMB,

AND A GENEROUS AND INSPIRING FRIEND,

I DEDICATE THESE POEMS

ST. ALBANS,
August, 1910.

PREFACE

OF the poems collected in this volume five have appeared in *The English Review*, one in *The Neolith*, two in *The Academy*, and the bulk of the remainder in *Vanity Fair*, under the editorship of Mr. Frank Harris. I am obliged to the editors and proprietors of these periodicals for permission to reproduce these poems in book form.

H. S.

RICHARD MIDDLETON

A MEMORY

ALTHOUGH most of Richard Middleton's work appeared in various journals of his day, it is not surprising that his name is still practically unknown. The end doubtless would have been served by the publication of a book in his lifetime but, this apart, few people are interested in poetry and very few know poetry when they see it. He was, again, poor, and but for certain friends with a more or less deep sense of his value " the adventure of literature" would have been even more difficult. Occasional articles and reviews for The Academy *were followed by more settled work on* Vanity Fair, *in which paper were published many of his poems. Later, he resumed his earlier connection and wrote also for* The English Review. *The last nine months of his life he spent in Brussels, dying there at the age of twenty-nine.*

He was of striking appearance. His unfashionable thick beard and long hair, his massive, deeply lined forehead and fine eyes, compelled attention, but to me at least he is chiefly memorable for a certain air of simple dignity and sense of self-respect. In earlier days intolerant of fools, he grew to be more patient, and, had he lived, would, I think, have suffered fools gladly. The genuine kindness, the gentleness and benignity of the man latterly were remarkable. Under his cares and almost isolated as he was in Brussels the old pagan spirit of the poems was changing, he was becoming more humane. In one of his later letters, "I grow a little warmer," he wrote, "to men and women in general;" and in another letter, "I feel drawn towards young children and people who are simple and kindly and not too clever. They give me a glimpse of the life that I have missed in my passionate search for enjoyment." Certainly he would not have written any more poems like his "Irene." Indeed, in his last year he wrote scarcely any poetry at all, devoting himself to prose.

With his contemporaries he had but little in common. They were, he considered, for the most part propagandists—"propagartists" he called them—moralists, reformers, anything but what he would have had them be, lovers of Beauty. Of the poets he at one time greatly admired Mr. A. E. Housman, but admitted later that the "distinctive bitter flavour" of "The Shropshire Lad" was against its "being of the highest quality." Mr. Kenneth

*Grahame is the author with whom he was most in
sympathy. When his essays are collected it will be found
that he shares with Mr. Grahame and Stevenson the rare
gift of evoking the thoughts and feelings of childhood.
With young people he was always on terms of equality.
Hearing of his death, " I cannot possibly tell the children,"
wrote a friend. "We all had a real affection for him, and
here he was always at his best."*

*Such was the man. Of his genius I am not using words
idly when I say that it is of that rare quality which
will sooner or later ensure him a recognised position
in the front rank of English poets. Those who are not
moved by the beauty of the poetry in this volume may
find beauty elsewhere and had better seek it elsewhere.
There is that in it beyond the reach of mere criticism.
It is of that substance which lives.*

HENRY SAVAGE.

CONTENTS

CONTENTS

CONTENTS

CONTENTS

POEMS AND SONGS

IN MEMORIAM

Now, in this sombre and regretful place,
  Grey when the sun has crimsoned all the west,
With sorrow like a mask upon my face,
  I lay my dreams to rest.

Poor dreams that are as many as my days,
  Poor days that are as many as my dreams,
The spring once gave you all his roundelays,
  The harvest moon her beams.

This one was wet with delicate grey rain,
  And this sang ballads to an amber moon ;
And this set tender harmonies of pain
  To a delicious tune.

All fallen into dust—Ah, God ! that I
  Had stayed unknowing in my first glad bed,
If thus beneath the drear and desolate sky,
  I had not laid my dead.

CHANT—PAGAN

Lay down your sword of thunder,
You little gods of wonder!
  We have sought young Love in the world above,
And the earth is rent asunder.
By lightning you may blind him,
And in his darkness bind him,
  By flower and sod, on the steps of God,
We shall seek young Love and find him.

And heaven's dimmest rafter
Shall tremble to our laughter,
  While we leave our tears to your hopeless years,
Though there be nothing after;
And while your day uncloses
Its lorn and tattered roses,
  We shall pluck the stars from your prison bars
And bind celestial posies.

An hour to heap our treasure,
And tread our careless measure,
  An hour of dreams where the rainbow gleams,
And the moonlight takes its pleasure.

CHANT—PAGAN

An hour to find what bliss is
In freer worlds than this is ;
    An hour to lie 'twixt earth and sky,
And conquer time with kisses.

Step down from your high places,
You gods of fallen races !
    By field and flood, our pagan blood
Shall mock you to your faces.
By craven fear begotten,
Your musty bones grow rotten,
    By night and day, when wise men pray,
Your creeds shall be forgotten.

No son of man shall fear you,
No woman shall come near you,
    Your lips may cry from your riven sky,
And the lovers shall not hear you.
Lay down your sword of thunder,
You little gods of wonder !
    We have sought our love in the world above,
And your veil is rent asunder.

THE BATHING BOY

I saw him standing idly on the brim
  Of the quick river, in his beauty clad,
So fair he was that Nature looked at him
    And touched him with her sunbeams here and
      there,
    So that his cool flesh sparkled, and his hair
  Blazed like a crown above the naked lad.

And so I wept; I have seen lovely things,
  Maidens and stars and roses all a-nod
In moonlit seas, but Love without his wings
    Set in the azure of an August sky,
    Was all too fair for my mortality,
  And so I wept to see the little god.

Till with a sudden grace of silver skin
  And golden lock he dived, his song of joy
Broke with the bubbles as he bore them in;
    And lo, the fear of night was on that place,
    Till decked with new-found gems and flushed
      of face,
  He rose again, a laughing, choking boy.

ON A DEAD CHILD

MAN proposes, God in His time disposes,
   And so I wandered up to where you lay,
A little rose among the little roses,
   And no more dead than they.

It seemed your childish feet were tired of straying,
   You did not greet me from your flower-strewn bed,
Yet still I knew that you were only playing—
   Playing at being dead.

I might have thought that you were really sleeping,
   So quiet lay your eyelids to the sky,
So still your hair, but surely you were peeping,
   And so I did not cry.

God knows, and in His proper time disposes,
   And so I smiled and gently called your name,
Added my rose to your sweet heap of roses,
   And left you to your game.

THE CAROL OF THE POOR CHILDREN

WE are the poor children, come out to see the
  sights
On this day of all days, on this night of nights,
The stars in merry parties are dancing in the sky,
A fine star, a new star, is shining on high !

We are the poor children, our lips are frosty blue,
We cannot sing our carol as well as rich folk do,
Our bellies are so empty we have no singing voice,
But this night of all nights good children must
  rejoice.

We do rejoice, we do rejoice, as hard as we can try,
A fine star, a new star is shining in the sky !
And while we sing our carol, we think of the delight
The happy kings and shepherds make in Bethlehem
  to-night.

Are we naked, mother, and are we starving-poor—
Oh, see what gifts the kings have brought outside the
  stable door,
Are we cold, mother, the ass will give his hay
To make the manger warm and keep the cruel winds
  away.

THE CAROL OF THE POOR CHILDREN

We are the poor children, but not so poor who sing
Our carol with our voiceless hearts to greet the new-
    born king,
On this night of all nights, when in the frosty sky
A new star, a kind star is shining on high !

THE UNKNOWN ROAD

THE road crept gaily from the town,
    And all the knights adventurous
Were riding up and riding down,
    Aye, all the gallant warriors,
Whose hopeful hearts may God befriend,
Along the road without an end.

Right well they fared, yet on the way,
    That young hearts all sing eagerly,
Were some who wrought in colours gay
    At painted boards and tapestries,
" This is the road to love," they said;
" And this the pavement of the dead."

The knights fell sad. " Which way," they cried,
    " Now may we go adventurous ?
Not to the courts of love we ride,
    Nor to the mouths of sepulchres ;
Not for our hearts were these things shown,
Which seek for God, the Great Unknown."

8

THE UNKNOWN ROAD

Now they about their eyes have tied
    The scarves of youth invincible,
And down the laughing road they ride,
    In places dark and dangerous,
Seeking the ways no man has trod,
To justify their swords to God.

And so it seems the thing doth fare,
    With men of mind adventurous,
The critics labour everywhere
    With cunning hand unwavering,
What time, regardless of their light,
The poets wonder in the night.

THE LAST CRUISE

THE stars were out overhead, and "Lo!" I cried,
  "Nevermore,
    Nevermore shall the palace know me;" and high
      on the masts
The white sails trembled as skyward the good ship
  bore
        Her cargo of shadows.
Never a word of regret as I stood on her moonlit
  poop
    And sang not of old past things but of wonders
      to be;
And saw great birds with a glory of plumage swoop
    Down the sea's meadows.

Ah! the wind on my forehead that might not blow
    on the earth,
  Surely the gates were open, and I might forget
The quiet eyes of the past that seemed life's worth,
      That were but seeming.
I saw the lights of a ship march slowly over the sea,
  And the land fell away behind me, and into the
    night
That covereth all things and passeth no more for me,
      My heart went dreaming.

THE SONG OF THE KING'S MINSTREL

I SING no longer of the skies,
And the swift clouds like driven ships,
For there is earth upon my eyes
And earth between my singing lips.
Because the King loved not my song
That he had found so sweet before,
I lie at peace the whole night long,
And sing no more.

The King liked well my song that night;
Upon the palace roof he lay
With his fair Queen, and as I might
I sang, until the morning's grey
Crept o'er their faces, and the King,
Mocked by the breaking dawn above,
Clutched at his youth and bade me sing
A song of love.

Well it might be—the King was old,
And though his Queen was passing fair,
His dull eyes might not catch the gold
That tangled in her wayward hair.

THE SONG OF THE KING'S MINSTREL

It had been much to see her smile,
  But with my song I made her weep.
Our heavens last but a little while,
  So now I sleep.

More than the pleasures that I had
  I would have flung away to know
My song of love could make her sad,
  Her sweet eyes fill and tremble so.
What were my paltry store of years,
  My body's wretched life to stake,
Against the treasure of her tears,
  For my love's sake ?

Not lightly is a King made wise,
  My body ached beneath his whips,
And there is earth upon my eyes,
  And earth between my singing lips.
But I sang once—and for that grace
  I am content to lie and store
The vision of her dear, wet face,
  And sing no more.

THE REBEL

I AM the man who wandered in the skies,
  To a strange place hung round with flowing silk
    Wherein were set the stars from north to south;
And there I saw a god with dreamy eyes,
  And monstrous shadowing beard that dripped with
    milk,
    And there was honey on his drooping mouth.

Then I rejoiced to see him newly fed,
  Because his forehead shone without a fold,
    While his vast chest beat out the pulse of
    years;
"I come for tidings of the newly dead!"
  I cried, and flung before him all my gold,
    And all my pitiful prayings, and my tears.

The god dreamed on, and all about him swayed
  The starry tapestries, and in their deep
    I saw new planets quicken and burn dim;
But I had loved and I was unafraid,
  And while the fat god panted in his sleep
    And snorted centuries, I hated him.

THE REBEL

"Will you not wake, oh god, because he calls
  Who for your sake has knelt beneath the sky,
    And for the sake of her but newly dead?"
But still the stars held mazy festivals,
  And universes throbbed melodiously,
    And still the god down-drooped his drowsy
    head.

And so, because he would not heed my prayer,
  I turned on him with laughter as he lay,
    And mocked him for a wittol to his face ;
And laughing swept the field of heaven bare,
  And as the long night trembled into day
    I set myself upon a throne in space.

THE FLOWER-GIRL

I STAND here all the day,
  Calling my roses,
    Under a sunny sky,
    "Oh! will you buy
  My pretty posies—
My lords and ladies gay?"

Thirteen summers are dead
  With all their roses,
    Now cry I down the street,
    "Oh! buy my sweet
  My pretty posies!
My flowers white and red."

The wind sings all the day
  Swaying my roses,
    "Oh! come, my little one!
    Come, heed the sun
  And drop your posies!
My little one and play——"

THE FLOWER-GIRL

I bend my weary head
　Down to my roses,
　　"He would not be unkind,
　　The gentle wind,
　My pretty posies—
But oh! that I were dead!"

And still I stand all day
　Calling my roses,
　　So old, so old am I,
　　"Oh! will you buy
　My pretty posies—
My lords and ladies gay?"

LULLABY

Ah little one, you're tired of play,
  Sleep's fingers rest upon your brow,
You've been a woman all the day
  You'd be a baby now ;
    Oh baby, my baby !
  You'd be my baby now.

Perhaps you had forgotten me
  Because the daisies were so white.
But now you come to mother's knee,
  My little babe to-night ;
    Oh baby, my baby !
  My baby every night.

To-morrow when the sun's awake
  You'll seek your flowery fields again.
But night shall fall, and for my sake
  You'll be a baby then ;
    Oh baby, my baby !
  My little baby then.

17

LULLABY

And you'll grow big and love will call
  Happen you'll leave me for your man,
And night-times when the shadows fall
  I'll greet as mothers can ;
    Oh baby, my baby !
  As only mothers can.

And now my little heart of May,
  Lie closely, sleep is on your brow,
You've been a woman all the day,
  You'd be my baby now ;
    Oh baby, my baby !
  My little baby now.

ADRIFT

OH the days, the angry days,
Hot on all the watery ways,
And the nights that gave us only
Stars, to make the whole world lonely!

Weary heart and weary head,
All too weary to be dead,
We as children seeking shadows
Danced along the sea's green meadows.

Always would the hours unfold
Endless days of ghastly gold,
And the sun that might not pity
Triumphed o'er a golden city.

Where we wandered maze on maze,
Street on street of heat and haze,
Sung by bells in every quarter,
And their song was "Water! Water!"

We with black and muttering lips
Called to dreamy far-off ships,
When they passed, we, peering after,
Cackled forth in dreamy laughter.

ADRIFT

Till time vanished and hope done,
And beneath the raging sun
Our shrunk bodies blazed and embered,
Lo! a sail : God had remembered

Oh the days, the empty days,
Down along the watery ways,
And the nights that gave us only
Stars, to make the whole world lonely.

TO LILY

THE black trees lean towards their starry God
   And murmur to me in the dreamy light,
   While I stoop down to pluck the lilies white
That grow wherever your glad feet have trod,
   Oh my belovèd! my song is of the night.

Cool on my forehead underneath the sky
   The soft wind blows, and in the dew-wet grass
   The lilies cluster where your feet did pass,
Cluster and dance to me but never die,
   For I have borne them to my treasury.

Even to my fair treasury of dreams,
   Where all I have of you is garnered fast,
   Moonlit and sunlit lilies of the past
Spoil of dead stars, to speak of love it seems
   Even in that great dream which is the last.

For they shall sway about me in that place
   Wherein my soul shall lay my body down,
   And all along the streets of Death's grey town
Their scent shall bear remembrance of your grace,
   And where they triumph I shall see your face.

TO LILY

Oh my belovèd ! my song is of the night,
  The quiet night with dewy eyes that weep
For very gladness on the lilies white
Which cluster in the dreams of my delight,
  And whisper love across the hills of sleep

THE GLAD NIGHTS OF SPRING

WE are the men who make the world a song
  For all the children of the world to sing,
  We are the lonely rulers of the spring
Dreaming upon our thrones the whole night long
  Till high upon the eastern hills there glows
  The summer, like a rose.

And while in dim forgotten graves there sleep
  If God grant, lightly, those who long ago
  Danced to the loving winds of spring, they know
That on the dying hours our watch we keep
  To welcome back across the midnight airs
  No other love than theirs.

Her voice is like the song of hidden streams
  Laughing at dusk, her feet are wet with dew,
  Her eyes are set with God's eternal blue.
She is the perfect lady of our dreams,
  And far across the night and far and far
  We seek her like a star.

THE GLAD NIGHTS OF SPRING

There is no resting-place for tired head
   Like her soft breasts, there is no love like hers,
   And ever on her gentle lips there stirs
The triumphing song that comforted the dead,
   Over their graves the dewy trees shine wet,
   But they may not forget.

We are the rulers of the quiet hours
   Who love where loved the dead, and in our hands
   We hold the keys of fair, untrodden lands,
Where summer comes not to perplex the flowers,
   But spring stays ever, and spring music fills
   The dark and dreamy hills.

TO DOROTHY

THE night has sprinkled all the woods with dew,
  Stars wink in grassy places, and the trees
Bend down their sodden mournful heads where—
    through
  Rare night-birds thrill their harsh discordancies.
And far upon the silent hills there roll
  Strange shapes of mist, and soft bewildered things
  Beat on my shrinking face with noisome wings,
But there are noonday revels in my soul.

Beyond the sombre woods your window shines
  Gold for the night and morning for my eyes,
And to my passion love's enchanted wines
  Have touched with crimson all the midnight skies.
When far across the dismal earth there steals
  Your sunlit sweetness, there were no more day,
  Though from his beaten pavements far away
The summer sun drove his fierce chariot wheels.

Oh, love! look forth, for I have crossed the night,
  The bitter night, full many a weary mile,
I have made careless songs for your delight
  And plucked my dreams apart to dare your smile.

25

TO DOROTHY

I have flung all my treasure in your way
   That it might thrill to dust beneath your feet,
   But night is near me now, and, oh, my sweet,
My very love! look forth and give me day.

TO C. M.

DEAR dreamer, with the wonderful wide eyes,
  You are not mine to love, nor may I know
Under what star, beneath what passionate skies,
  Your feet exulting go.
But I have seen your eyes made bold with tears
And love, rebuke the rebellious hemispheres.

I know I am as nothing in your place
  Of sombre love and strange, magnificent flowers,
But I have loosed your hair about my face
  To witch my midnight hours ;
And I have dreamed that your sweet tears are shed
On me at dawn when I bring forth my dead.

My feet across the threshold of your shrine,
  Whence your love's incense to the stars is curled,
May wander not, but for this peace of mine,
  Oh, laugh away my world !
And let me see beneath the enchanted skies,
Spring and your lover hold their revelries.

TO C. M.

Oh, let me hear you speak to him, and share
   Though none of mine, the reticent, sweet song
That charms your sleep-bound courts and cities where
   Your glad dream-courtiers throng,
To greet across the vision-pavèd ways,
Your star-lit nights, your fair, desirous days.

There is a bitterness in love for me,
   For every kiss shall burn my flesh with fire,
I am a prince of thwarted ecstasy,
   Of unassuaged desire.
Yet would I know your new-bewitched skies,
Dear dreamer, and your passionate, wide eyes.

CHRISTINE

How cold she is! and yet that shade of her
Who fills my dreams with sensuous images
Has veins of warmer, quicker blood than these
Who yield me their affections.   Might I stir
The secret pool that is her heart, and·blur
With ringèd ripples the tranquillities,
Which are a deathly glass to one who sees
His own swart soul, where truth and wonder were—
Would Love unfold his wings, and fan my face
With odorous winds of dreams made animate
And wondered things become the things that are,
Or should I turn and seek another place,
While from the broken halls and desolate
She wandered forth to greet the morning star?

TO H. S.

LOVE is life's enemy, for we who hold
  Within our dreams our passionate carouse,
Count not dawn's silver or the sunset's gold,
  Winning dim jewels for our vision-house.
While all the noontide blossoms lose their scent
  And all life's flowers droop their faded heads,
  We gather roses from celestial beds
And lilies from the starlit firmament.

And being born of dreams they shall not die,
  For though the dreamers perish, these shall wake
Earth, with their fragrant immortality,
  And on the hills their lovely buds shall break ;
While of our dreams new lovers' dreams shall be,
  And in our night-time they shall find their rest,
  Watching the sun pass down into the west
Stained by the wine of our old ecstasy.

We saw the new-made stars dance forth above,
  And we shall see them flicker out and die,
We are but moments in the tide of love,
  Yet are we one with love's eternity.

TO H. S.

And when the Immortal wearies of His moods
    And is no more, our song shall capture still
    The place of timeless silences, and fill
With grateful rapture the cold solitudes.

AT THE GATES

How long, how long, oh, night?
  The delicate fabric of the stars is frayed
Where dawn lets in the light;
  And, in the scented glade,
The thrushes thread day's lattices, and sing
The end of your impassioned sorrowing.

I see your glittering tears
  Scattered upon the lawn's awaking green;
The bitter knowledge of the bitter years
  Since ever love has been,
Lies in your deep, kind breast, and with the day
You mourn poor human love, that dies alway.

How long, how long, oh, night?
  Across your hours
I have fulfilled the task of my delight,
  I have won rapturous lethargy of flowers;
But day unfolds, and I shall keep my song
How long, oh, night, oh, wanton love, how long?

UNDER THE WHIP

It well may be that death is God's last boon,
  For with the hours life's tapestry is blurred
  To strange, unshapen nothings ; I have heard
Eve in the twilight singing to the moon
The passionate song that has no human tune,
  And some fierce echo in my bosom stirred,
  Greeting the cry, as an imprisoned bird
The piping of the day. Oh Death, be soon !

For there is nothing left in life but this,
  And to this scarlet shrine is beauty fled
  Since Paradise grew earth and men were wise ;
But who can breathe beneath your final kiss,
  Love ! and who would not rather be well dead
  Than feed the torment in your laughing eyes !

THE BALLAD OF THE BACCHANALS

WHILE yet above the western hills
  The sun was red, they came to me
And cried, "Your fame the city fills
  For cunning song and minstrelsy,
And at your peril it were well
  To bring us, ere to-morrow falls,
A song new fashioned out of hell
  To crown our autumn Bacchanals."

They passed; the sun went down like flame,
  And from her high acropolis
The queen of all the kisses came
  To quench my loving avarice.
She kissed my singing lips away,
  I cried, "Oh love! whate'er befalls,
I have a song to sing ere day,
  A song to crown the Bacchanals."

Now far above our loving-place
  Rode forth the star-accoutred Night,
And by her side I saw the face
  Of Sleep, her tender acolyte.

THE BALLAD OF THE BACCHANALS

In some high arbour of the moon
  We held our wanton festivals;
And wonder set our lips atune
  To crown the autumn Bacchanals.

While yet upon her lips I lay
  Dreaming in exquisite suspense,
I saw the chariot of day
  Across the eastern battlements.
And cried, "Oh! truly love is long,
  For even now the daylight calls,
And for my love I have no song
  To crown the autumn Bacchanals."

But she said, "For my beauty's sake
  Anoint my soul with kisses yet,
This is a better song we make
  Than any that the gods forget!"
And while the accursed sun up-climbed
  To steal the stars, the city walls,
Our loving hearts exulting rhymed
  The Ballad of the Bacchanals.

They led us forth beneath the sky,
  The abundant earth would have its own,
And yet it was not hard to die
  With love for a companion.

THE BALLAD OF THE BACCHANALS

They led us forth towards the sea,
And there beyond the city walls,
We sang beneath the gallows tree
The Ballad of the Bacchanals.

THE PIRATE SHIP

WE fought her in the dark until her spars
  Touched the black heart of night with fairy gold,
And she flung largesse to the pitying stars,
  The fragrant incense of her teeming hold.
It seemed as though the very sea was glad
  Decking its bosom with a thousand gems,
While the air swarmed with fireflies dancing mad
  About her masts' enchanted diadems.

Upon our decks the dead men watched the sky
  With wonder in their faces, and her crew
Cursed in the shadows of their misery
  The sombre wind that to the gallows blew.
While from the torment of the sanguine smoke
  One called on Pity by her tender name,
Until across the disordered sea there broke
  The light of morning, bitter sick with flame.

Our cheeks were pale, the blood upon our hands
  Crumbled to purple dust, our tired eyes
Held visions of our pleasant meadow-lands
  Leaping to day beneath the Kentish skies.

37

THE PIRATE SHIP

No new wind soothed strained brow and bitten lip,
  The morning lay upon us for a shroud,
While o'er the sea, the ember of a ship
  Breathing thin smoke, passed landwards like a cloud.

    .   .   .   .   .

Last eve across a mad encrimsoned sea
  I saw the sun plunge down into the night
Even as a flaming vessel, and on me
  There fell the glory of an ancient fight.

NEW LOVE

THE boy weeps in the wild woods,
  His bright eyes are sore,
The old inhuman solitudes
  May shield his heart no more ;
A maid has happened out of hell
And kissed his crimson lips too well.

Where may he hide his miseries ?
  Where quench the lips that burn
For scarlet love ? the tangled trees,
  Bramble and gorse and fern
Can hide him not, nor may he cool
His mouth in any forest pool.

Love laughs about the groves of pine,
  Pan wantons in the glade,
And the boy is drunk with a new wine,
  And the boy's heart is afraid ;
Her lips were soft and very kind,
Her breath was like a summer wind.

NEW LOVE

Oh ! wanton night, made glad with dew,
  Hung with a starry veil !
The boy is lost for loving you,
  The old enchantments fail.
You have led his feet to hell's gate—
To a crimson dawn and passionate.

No more in leafy solitudes,
  God's pavèd fields among,
He shall win the peace of the wild woods
  With the joy of his quiet song.
For love has found the groves of pine,
And the boy is drunk with a new wine.

ON A DEAD YOUTH

THE boy dreams . . .
Lays down before his God a rosebud's worth,
And far above the shrine a planet gleams ;
No more of earth !
And at his side the maidens may not weep,
Lest it should break his sleep.

All his spring flowers beneath their feet lie dead,
Dear boy, and love was never a word he used,
Though for their faces all his tears were shed
And all his roses bruised ;
Better it was, ere shame were kissed awake
To perish for their sake.

And with soft fingers they shall pity death
And close his lovely eyes,
And they shall warm his body with their breath,
Stir heaven with their sighs ;
For life shall give them other lips to kiss,
But none so sweet as this.

ON A DEAD YOUTH

And then with mournful wonder they shall go,
Love's wings are furled,
And well they know that they shall never know
The meaning of the world,
But some dim thing within their bosom cries,
And Adonais dies.

The boy dreams . . .
Why should we weep for him who wakes no more?
The kisses shall not burn for him, it seems,
The frail heart's core;
Though on the hills the lonely maidens call,
Love, to his festival.

TO IRENE

I THINK the earth was dead last night, for I,
   Keeping you in my arms could feel no breath
   From all the slumbrous trees, it seemed that death
Had wooed the fields, for in our ecstasy
They had no part and where the thrushes flew
   In drowsy autumn, now no creature moved
   Across the fallen leaves, save where we loved,
And there I heard faint wings discover you.

And then you thrilled with some supreme desire
   That was not of my dreams, your pulses beat
   Time to the world, and with rebellious feet
Your triumphing passions scaled the gates of fire ;
And lo, I was as dust ! in some far place
   My soul paid tribute to tremendous kings,
   Who bowed their head before your gleaming wings
And praised your beauty with averted face.

Love is too great for me, from this dead world
   Wherein I hold a child's uncertainties,
   I may not dare the glamour of his skies
Scatheless, nor see his magic wings unfurled.

TO IRENE

The dead men clamour round me and I know
I am no more than they, who may not keep
The secret hours that are too glad for sleep
With love that stays and dreams that laughing go.

THE HAPPY CRUISE

WHERE silver waters flow,
  We cool our burning lips,
  And where the honey drips
Upon the earth below
From flowers white with snow,
  We load our dreamy ships,
  Till when the red sun dips,
Stars blossom, thus we go !

The girls are flushed with wine,
  And singing in the shade,
  And wanton words invade
Their delicate mouths that pine
Through kissing of the vine,
  And every golden maid
  Loves, though she be betrayed,
The stars, the stars that shine.

Gladly the rigging sings,
  But, oh ! how glad are we,
  Lords of the dreaming sea,
And of delicious things ;

THE HAPPY CRUISE

We are more rich than kings,
  Or any men that be,
  While down eternity,
We beat with shadowy wings.

And thus our watch we keep,
  Upon the summer sky ;
  Lives fade and droop and die,
And yet we do not weep,
Who sail the starry deep,
  With but one human cry,
  "Quietly, quietly,
The girls are all asleep ! "

DUST OF DREAMS

THE moon across the world of gentler light
  Down to the morning drives her starry teams ;
While I enrich the treasury of night
  With purple robes and jewels wrought in dreams ;
For while upon the dying hours I keep
  My sleepless watch, upon my soul there falls
Rest beyond rest, sleep that is more than sleep,
  Love, from your castle walls.

And through the hours of night the jewelled foam
  Torn by the winds from the adventurous seas,
Flies back before my galleons driving home
  To heap their treasure on the magic quays.
I may not sleep till high upon their spars
  I see the pale hand of the morning gleam,
I need not sleep for love has won the stars
  To make the world my dream.

Oh love ! oh dream ! if ever I awake
  In some sad place of life, may I arise
And win forgetfulness for your sweet sake,
  And dare the night once more with open eyes ;

DUST OF DREAMS

With open eyes and cold, and heaven above
  Shall know I do not dream though yet I store
Dream beyond dream, love that is more than love,
  Mine, till I dream no more.

TEARS

IF these be tears that fill my eyes
  With rumour of a thousand stars
  Until my tired mind unbars
Its sombre portals to the skies,
To find in each enchanted light
  That thrills along the heavenly way
  A golden glory more than day,
A wonder far beyond the night——

Weep on, oh heart! it well may be
  That these sad eyes were made to weep,
  To find what others find in sleep
Within a teardrop's brilliancy,
And it may be these pools of fire
  That earth and sea and heaven guard,
  Shall prove my ultimate reward
The jewels that surpass desire.

THE SONG OF THE GLAD WOMAN

I saw a boy, a pretty boy,
  Who wandered in the woodlands wild;
It made my bosom leap for joy
  To see the child, the lovely child.
And yet he wept and would not play,
  And all the birds made moan above,
With well-a-day and well-a-day,
  Ah! well-a-day for love.

I held him to my yearning breast,
  And with my pity lulled his fears;
And there he lay and took his rest,
  While on my face there fell his tears.
They burned my beauty quite away,
  Till all the birds made moan above,
With well-a-day and well-a-day
  Ah! well-a-day for love.

No morning dew can heal the smart
  Where fell his kisses on my brow;
He weeps no more upon my heart—
  It is my heart that's weeping now.

THE SONG OF THE GLAD WOMAN

He was so sweet he might not stay,
   And all the birds make moan above,
With well-a-day and well-a-day,
   Ah ! well-a-day for love.

Yet I rejoice that in an hour
   I saw the boy, the pretty boy ;
For he has given me the power
   That out of sorrow bringeth joy.
And so I shall not him gainsay,
   Though all the birds make moan above,
With well-a-day and well-a-day,
   Ah ! well-a-day for love.

AUTUMNAL

Across the scented garden of my dreams
  Where roses grew, Time passes like a thief,
Among my trees his silver sickle gleams,
  The grass is stained with many a ruddy leaf;
And on cold winds the petals float away
That were the pride of June and her array.

The bare boughs weave a net upon the sky
  To catch Love's wings and his fair body bruise;
There are·no flowers in the rosary—
  No song-birds in the mournful avenues;
Though on the sodden air not lightly breaks
The elegy of Youth, whom love forsakes.

Ah, Time! one flower of all my garden spare,
  One rose of all the roses, that in this
I may possess my love's perfumèd hair
  And all the crimson secrets of her kiss.
Grant me one rose that I may drink its wine,
And from her lips win the last anodyne.

AUTUMNAL

For I have learnt too many things to live,
  And I have loved too many things to die;
But all my barren acres I would give
  For one red blossom of eternity,
To animate the darkness and delight
The spaces and the silences of night.

But dreams are tender flowers that in their birth
  Are very near to death, and I shall reap,
Who planted wonder, unavailing earth,
  Harsh thorns and miserable husks of sleep.
I have had dreams, but have not conquered Time,
And love shall vanish like an empty rhyme.

DREAM SONG

I COME from woods enchaunted,
Starlit and pixey-haunted,
  Where 'twixt the bracken and the trees
  The goblins lie and take their ease
By winter moods undaunted.

There down the golden gravel
The laughing rivers travel ;
  Elves wake at nights and whisper low
  Between the bracken and the snow
Their dreamings to unravel.

Twisted and lank and hairy,
With wanton eyes and wary,
  They stretch and chuckle in the wind,
  For one has found a mermaid kind,
And one has kissed a fairy.

They know no melancholy,
But fashion crowns of holly,
  And gather sleep within the brake
  To deck a kingdom when they wake,
And bless the dreamer's folly.

DREAM SONG

Ah! would that I might follow
The servants of Apollo!
  But it is sweet to heap the hours
  With quiet dreams and poppy-flowers,
Down in the pixies' hollow.

FOR HE HAD GREAT POSSESSIONS

Ah ! marvel not if when I come to die
  And follow Death the way my fancies went
Year after fading year, the last mad sky
  Finds me impenitent ;
For though my heart went doubting through the
    night,
  With many a backward glance at heaven's face,
Yet found I many treasures of delight
  Within this pleasant place.

I shall not grieve because the girls were fair
  And kinder than the world, nor shall I weep
Because with crying lips and clinging hair
  They stole away my sleep.
For lacking this I might not yet have known
  How high the heart could climb, or waking seen
The mountains bare their silver breasts of stone
  From their chaste robes of green.

Though it were all a sin, within the mirth
  And pain of life I found a song above
Our songs, in her who scattered on the earth
  Her glad largesse of love ;

56

FOR HE HAD GREAT POSSESSIONS

As though she held some dream that was not ours
   In some far place that was not for our feet,
Where blew across the gladder, madder flowers
   A wind more bitter-sweet.

Ah ! who shall hearten when the music stops,
   For joy of silence ? While they dreamed above
She showed me love upon the mountain tops
   And in the valleys, love.
And while the wise found heaven with their charts
   And lore of souls, she made an earth for me
More sweet than all, and from our beating hearts
   She called the pulsing sea.

So marvel not if in the days when death
   Shall make my body mine, I do not cry
For hours and treasure lost, but with my breath
   Praise my mortality.
For lo ! this place is fair, and losing all
   That I have won and dreamed beneath her kiss,
I would not see the light of morning fall
   On any world but this.

LAMENT FOR LILIAN

I BOW my head before the hands of Fate
  And dream no more and reap no more of song.
  I have denied my destiny too long,
I have achieved my punishment too late;
For I, in vanished, unforgotten hours,
    Such little hands, such shining eyes, have known,
    That, lacking these, I may not sing alone
In this sad place of salt and withered flowers.

And this is life—and these, dear God, are men,
    These pale, thin shades!   Long since by my dream's
      grace
    The dawn wind blew her hair across her face,
And there was rapture in the morning then.
Her eyes shone darkly in the silken net
    Flung slantwise o'er her face, her glad lips said,
    "You will remember Lily when she's dead."
And this is life—would God I might forget!

Beneath her feet the green earth rolled away
    From sea to sea, and I might understand
    The water's song, the music of the land,
The lingering choruses of night and day,

LAMENT FOR LILIAN

That gave me, with a dole of childish tears,
  The knowledge of my blood's supreme delight:
  The yearning of the morning for the night,
The timeless passion of the hemispheres.

My love was more than any life of mine
  And more than me, before its sudden gleam
  The years that knew me faded like a dream,
I was as one who drinks enchanted wine
To sport with gods ; and yet there shone for me
  Across my madness, Lily, laughingwise,
  A human blossom glad for human eyes,
Made pagan by a child's serenity.

Ah! Lord of Love, these are my eyes that weep,
  These are my lips that do lament her so,
  Mourning the little feet that long ago
Made echoes, echoes, in the halls of sleep,
With such delight of dance as children keep
  When spring has strewed the daisy-fields with snow,
  To such soft music as the children know
Greeting the spring, upon the hills a-peep.

If she were dead, surely in dreamy ways
  Her tender spirit would delight me still,
  With gifts of lilies, tall and fair, and fill
With silver blossoms my unhappy days.

LAMENT FOR LILIAN

And through the meadows where the moon a-stir
  Binds the wet flowers in garlands with her beams
  To deck the brows of sleep, across my dreams,
Down to the morning I would follow her.

For I am lord of all fair things that Death
  Has fashioned into dreams, and all his art
  Would only bring more surely to my heart
My wondrous Lily, sweet with flowers' breath,
Who now, in alien palaces, enchaunts
  Youth, with her laughing lips and shining eyes,
  And treads no more beneath the summer skies
The sombre forests that Apollo haunts.

Song is no tribute to a singing girl,
  For whom the wanton earth makes madrigals,
  To whom each wistful star at twilight calls
In tuneful numbers from the heavenly whirl;
So here's an end, I ask forgetfulness
  Now that my little store of hours is spent,
  And heart to laugh upon my punishment—
Dear God, what means a poet more or less?

PAGAN EPITAPH

Servant of the eternal Must
  I lie here, here let me lie,
In the ashes and the dust,
  Dreaming, dreaming pleasantly.
When I lived I sought no wings,
  Schemed no heaven, planned no hell,
But, content with little things,
  Made an earth, and it was well.

Song and laughter, food and wine,
  Roses, roses red and white,
And a star or two to shine
  On my dewy world at night.
Lord, what more could I desire?
  With my little heart of clay
I have lit no eternal fire
  To burn my dreams on Judgment Day!

Well I loved, but they who knew
  What my laughing heart could be,
What my singing lips could do,
  Lie a-dreaming here with me.

PAGAN EPITAPH

I can feel their finger-tips
  Stroke the darkness from my face,
And the music of their lips
  Fills my pleasant resting-place
In the ashes and the dust,
  Where I wonder as I lie,
Servant of the eternal Must,
  Dreaming, dreaming pleasantly.

DAWN-LOVE

Not with my lips, O God, not with my eager hands
These purple seas were made and these enchanted
    lands,
It was not I who drew these breezes forth
And called these stars to diadem the north,
It was not I who set her in this place,
And in a dream of dreams decreed her face.

I only stoop to serve her careless days,
Bid the loud birds sing gladder roundelays
To charm her ears, and summer buds unfold
The crimson petals from their hearts of gold
To deck the earth her very feet have trod—
I sing the triumph of the Artist, God.

For when in dreams I wrought to make my heaven
    fair,
Raised palaces of song and minarets of prayer,
Domes of desire and secret halls of sin,
There was no vision walked my courts within
Like this, through all my twilit halls there blew
No song like this that burns my whole heart through

DAWN-LOVE

Down dreams, upon your knees, and pray to her
To touch your weary eyes! Let no dream stir
Till she has passed—she is so kind, so wild,·
So womanly, so very much a child,
That she can make a living thing of sleep,
Granting it lips to laugh and starry eyes to weep.

And she has made a living thing of me;
I feel the surge of earth, the rhythm of the sea,
My heart is freshened with the dewy rains
Of dawn, the sunshine burns within my veins;
For me the riotous seasons are unfurled,
I am a grain of dust; I am the world.

I know I have not made this perfect thing,
Lord of a thousand songs, this song I cannot sing,
Lord of a thousand dreams, this is no dream of
      mine,
Master of many feasts, I may not taste this wine;
But on the hills the perfect song is born,
And I arise from sleep to greet the morn.

IRENE

I WAS a singer in the days when Pan
  Leapt through the roses in the month of June,
  And shook the petals down upon the noon ;
And through the quashy bracken-glades I ran,
Dreaming no word of how the world began,
  Nor grieving in the graveyards of the moon
  Where pedants lie—I had a pipe, a tune,
And the first pagan ecstasy of man.

There passed me in the pleasant forest-light
  Fair forms of lovers trembling into rose
  That was not of the sun, and no man knows
With what delirious tumult of delight
Their voices filled the branches, and the sight
  Of their fine rapture conquered all my woes,
  As I had bathed in that black stream that flows
Across the passionless paradise of night.

It seemed that life was but a game to dare,
  The forfeit only death, and wandering
  Across the piney hills they heard me fling
A heart of hopeful music on the air,

TO IRENE

And there were roses, roses everywhere,
  And birds of tuneful voice and shining wing
  To carry love to God, the lips of spring
Had made the mouth of summer very fair.

Love played with us beneath the laughing trees,
  We praised him for his eyes and silver skin,
  And for the little teeth that shone within
His ruddy lips; the bracken touched his knees,
Earth wrapped his body in her softest breeze,
  And through the hours that held no count of sin
  We kept his court, until above our din
Night westward drove her glittering argosies.

Oh, lovely days long dead! There falls on me
  In this dim world I may not understand
  An echo of your sweetness; in my hand
One frail, sad rose inspires eternity
With dreams that are no more, and from the sea
  That beats upon this grey perplexèd land,
  Blows rumour of some merry drunken band
That keeps your revels still in Arcady.

ONE SUMMER'S DAY

SHE lay and smiled upon the hours,
  While with his silver pipe of joy
  The river hurried on ; a boy
Had covered her with cuckoo-flowers.
She let them stay as though she knew
  They could not hide her cheek's glad red,
  It seemed that heaven was her bed
And these but stars to wander through.

Till with a little loving leap
  The river rose above the boat,
  It girdled round her silver throat
And kissed her laughing eyes asleep.
Her hair was loosed, upon the flood
  There fell a sun-enchanted veil
  The glad waves plucked, her cheeks grown pale
Tinged the quick waters with their blood.

The sun cast down his brightest beams
  Upon the world, to give the news :
  " Across the merry waves of Ouse
Ophelia steers her bark of dreams."

ONE SUMMER'S DAY

The birds took up the strain above
  And flung it to the dimmest star:
  "Oh, let us follow, follow far
The dear mad maid who died for love!"

Even to the grave, dear heart, but soon,
  Too soon, the song of morning dies,
  Too soon we lose in memories
The radiant peace of afternoon.
While yet the river sang beside
  That knew no word of fear or doubt,
  We heard the Bedford bells breathe out
The soft, sad song of eventide.

When I count up my hours of gold,
  These shall not be forgotten, sweet;
  And though Time trample with his feet
Roses and lilies manifold—
If I have choice of all that seems
  Most precious here, this boon I choose,
  To see once more on merry Ouse
Ophelia steer her bark of dreams.

LOVE'S MORTALITY

THE night of nights drew to its tardy close
And through the dew the lily soothed the rose
With words of love immortal,
Till from the golden and desirèd portal
The curtains of the night were plucked aside,
And dawn led forth my bride.

And forth she came with her young limbs and
    cool,
Her eyes more clear than any windless pool,
To dance across the day-time,
Crown weary life with garlands of her play-time,
And set a bud betwixt the lips of Death
That sweet might be his breath.

I know that luckless lovers do not die,
Fashioning trifles for eternity
Of golden moments broken,
Of sighs and tears and passionate words half-
    spoken,
They may not rest, but strew the bitter years
With their immortal tears.

LOVE'S MORTALITY

But swift upon my tired ears there fell
Rumour of moon-drunk, star-lit Philomel,
On magic copses flinging
Her song too amorous-sweet for human singing,
And praising ever to her leafy sky
Our glad mortality.

Winning the fierce fulfilment of my love,
Come Death! th' intolerable sky above
No more my heart shall cover;
Earth is too narrow for a happy lover
With planets in his heart and in his hands
Immeasurable lands.

Come, Death, and free me from these earthy walls
That heaven may hold our final festivals
The white stars trembling under!
I am too small to keep this passionate wonder
Within my human frame: I would be dead
That God may be our bed.

I feel her breath upon my eyes, her hair
Falls on me like a blessing, everywhere
I hear her warm blood leaping,
And life it seems is but a fitful sleeping,
And we but fretful shades that dreamed before,
That love, and are no more.

ANY LOVER, ANY LASS

WHY are her eyes so bright, so bright,
  Why do her lips control
The kisses of a summer night,
  When I would love her soul ?

God set her brave eyes wide apart
  And painted them with fire,
They stir the ashes of my heart
  To embers of desire.

Her lips so tenderly are wrought
  In so divine a shape,
That I am servant to my thought
  And can no wise escape.

Her body is a flower, her hair
  About her neck doth play ;
I find her colours everywhere,
  They are the pride of day.

Her little hands are soft, and when
  I see her fingers move
I know in very truth that men
  Have died for less than love.

ANY LOVER, ANY LASS

Ah, dear, live, lovely thing! my eyes
   Have sought her like a prayer;
It is my better self that cries
   " Would she were not so fair! "

Would I might forfeit ecstasy
   And find a calmer place,
Where I might undesirous see
   Her too desirèd face.

Nor find her eyes so bright, so bright,
   Nor hear her lips unroll
Dream after dream the lifelong night,
   When I would love her soul.

THE WELCOME

Against her coming I will make
  Brave chains of stars delight the trees,
And moonlit dew begem the brake
  And fire my verdant tapestries.
No lingering ray of sunlight mars
  The wonder of my solitudes.
Bewitch my shadowy fields, oh stars,
  And thou, oh moon, enchant my woods !

And now the rapturous hour draws near,
  Birds flutter in the leafy street,
Flowers raise their heads in sensuous fear
  That she may crush them with her feet.
With dew-blind eyes the roses weep,
  She comes—she will not come it seems ;
The air is sick with scent of sleep
  And dust of long-forgotten dreams.

From many a fair, enchanted grove
  The song-birds carol sweet and clear,
It is the very breath of love
  That stirs the charmèd atmosphere ;

73

THE WELCOME

And while blithe insects through the night
　　Go humming by on silken wings,
A deeper fulness of delight
　　Discovers all desirous things.

To-night I do not love alone,
　　The wind is lorn with amorous tunes,
And the pale lilies one by one
　　Grieve for the passion of dead noons ;
The roses touch and weep no more,
　　Casting their petals on the sod
In crimson sacrifice before
　　The altar of the sightless god.

And where Pan squanders with his court,
　　Love shall not spare the hornèd King,
With red lips drawn to wanton sport
　　And teeth to bite and hands to cling.
And where the wood-boys bathe and fling
　　Across the world their limbs made cool,
Love tarries with his alms-giving,
　　And there is trouble by the pool.

Now is my passionate lifetime's core,
　　My moments touch eternity,
And all the things I dreamed before
　　Shall blossom in my blood and die.

THE WELCOME

Once like a cloud of incense curled
  To some dim god, the veil shall pass,
Once I shall be the moving world
  Before I break and change to grass.

For this my mother blessed her pain,
  For this I wondered on her knees,
For this the sunshine and the rain,
  The green earth and the glowing seas,
Who blindly followed some far light
  That led me on through hopes and fears,
I shall fulfil my soul to-night
  And win a meaning for my years.

Sing on, oh birds, and thou, oh moon
  Bewitch my woods to greet my queen!
Death waits upon my life, and soon
  I shall be but by having been.
Stoop low, oh stars, and render brave
  My life as an enchanted bower,
That I may keep within my grave
  The gleam of my immortal hour!

THE LAST HOPE

To crown the festival
And tumult of the wine,
Oh, my belovèd, may there fall
Silence, the sweetest song of all
For tired ears like mine.

I crave an hour of rest—
No more—before I go,
The crimson rose upon your breast
Calls me, while on the mountain-crest
Dawn wantons in the snow.

Too tired to mock or weep
The world that I have missed,
Love, in your heaven let me sleep
An hour or two, before I keep
My unperturbèd tryst.

The day is for the young,
Night holds my heart in pawn ;
But though my broken songs are sung
I see across the hills far-flung
The pennons of the dawn.

A. C. M.

WHEN I breathe no more
  Scent of love-bound posies,
  And the August roses
    Let their petals fall,
When in my heart's core
  Dream on dream reposes,
  And my story closes
    Past recall ;

Heart, the winds that blow
  Lightly o'er my leisure
  Haply they shall measure
    My glad life-time here ;
Laughing, " Well we know
  Love was all his treasure,
  Pain and pride and pleasure,
    Hope and fear."

I by death made brave
  Shall not heed their blowing,
  Though the flowers are glowing
    That I praised above ;
Holding in my grave
  Seed too fair for sowing,
  Knowledge past all knowing,
    Thee, my love !

EPITHALAMIUM

These are his years, he will possess
  Your little flowers of white and red,
Your every sweet enchanted tress
  Will twine about him in his bed,
The vision of your loveliness
  Will comfort him till he is dead.

His hands will touch you, and your face
  Will feel his kisses while you sleep,
The sweetness of your shy embrace
  Will steal across the heavenly deep,
Where in a star-forsaken place
  I serve my foolish dreams, and weep.

Made free from doubt he need not fight
  To win the much-desirèd land,
Nor seek to pierce beyond the night
  That shrouds this waste of salt and sand,
Granting you, for your heart's delight,
  The love that you can understand.

EPITHALAMIUM

My heart its mortal form outwears,
  My moments to the winds are flung—
But now it seems these are his years,
  And being handsome, gallant, young,
He will not vex you with his tears
  Or sing such songs as I have sung.

But day and night and night and day
  His lips will tell the tales you know,
And you will find them new alway
  While on the lonely hills I go
Dreaming of wanton stars at play,
  And wishing it were better so.

The love that made you mine shall bear
  Harsh fruit before the end of this,
For in the darkness you shall hear
  An echo that is none of his,
And you will droop with sudden fear
  Beneath his fond, adulterous kiss.

And while across the world I move
  Paying sad tribute to the moon,
And breathing in her courts above
  The fatal music of our noon,
Lo ! you shall hear his words of love
  Trip lightly to my deathless tune.

79

EPITHALAMIUM

And you will know that once I set
   Your eyes with gleaming stars, and made
Your breasts of pearls and roses wet
   With morning's kisses, and betrayed
The setting sun that I might get
   Red for your cheeks that would not fade.

But he will kiss your lips, and say
   The thing you know your whole life long,
Day after night, night after day,
   No word of right, no word of wrong,
And you shall charm the hours away
   With the last echo of my song.

THE SILENT LOVER

I CANNOT sing, I have no words
  To love you, hate you, make you mine—
To win your ear like mating birds,
  To brim your veins with wanton wine ;
    But all my longing senses cry
    Their faltering, broken oratory.

My words rehearsed, my songs new sung,
  Are lost beneath this fierce suspense,
I cannot sound with human tongue
  My heart's insurgent eloquence,
    Now of your lips, now of your eyes,
    Now of your falling melodies !

I have no words, but Time shall prove
  This song of mine the best of all,
My lips shall be as Love's, for love
  Shall make their silence musical ;
    And on some rapt, enchanted night,
    They shall reveal my heart's delight.

LOVE'S FREEDOM

To feel her shrink beneath my touch, and keep
  An hour's unreason with the dancing moon;
  To bid my enchanted senses thrill and swoon,
To kiss and long for breath, and longing sleep;
Oh mad, white nights of old, why should I weep
  Your fallen hours? I hear the self-same tune
  Sung by the roses to an August noon,
That troubled once your star-bewildered deep.

This is not all of love, for more than this
  The purer breezes of this gentler land
Bless me and make me glad, where heaven is
  I see the palace of my mistress stand;
Love is no victim for a wanton's kiss,
  Nor shall he be imprisoned by her hand.

LAST YEAR'S LOVE

THE silver boy went down to meet the morn,
    His eyes were azure and his lips were red,
And golden tendrils did his brow adorn
    And mimic sunbeams round his laughing head ;
The misty meadows caught his cry of joy :
Oh, summer ! summer ! sang the silver boy.

She came to him across the dewy day,
    With ruddy cheeks and shapen breasts aglow,
And all the mountains flung their mists away
    To see how Love might greet the earth, and know
The song that is too sweet for mortal ears,
The song of songs that shall restore the years.

Riot of fountains, song of leaping streams,
    And sombre music through the stately pines
Quickened the breathless passion of their dreams,
    Their veins were fraught with such enchanted wines
As press Olympus' grapes, their lips were set
To their sweet task of kissing, kissing yet.

83

LAST YEAR'S LOVE

Oh, summer! summer! thou hast kissed him cold,
  His eyelids turn from loving, and his store
Of shaken ringlets lose their early gold
  And are as dust, his lips shall sing no more
Joy to the morn that calls him from his bed;
We knew no other love and he is dead!

There falls no echo from the dreaming trees,
  The moonlit meadows have forgot his song,
These flowers were his azure eyes, and these
  The crimson lips that summer knew too long;
Young Love is dead, but these his elegy,
These mindful blossoms, they shall never die!

THE UNSUCCESSFUL LOVER

WHY mourn the sweet you may not get,
  The love you cannot keep?
The world has fairer lasses yet
  For boys who do not weep.
    To-morrow's kisses shall repay
    All that you love and lose to-day.

"Her eyes are brighter than the moon!"
  They do not shine for you—
"Her lips with their enchanted tune
  Have made the world anew!"
    But what's the use of lips like this,
    Mad lover, if they will not kiss?

"I would have taught her soon or late."
  Now many a son of man
Better instruct his ordered fate
  To choose another plan,
    Or guide the stars through heaven above,
    Than teach a woman how to love.

THE UNSUCCESSFUL LOVER

Go out, oh, boy, across the earth ;
  The girls are there to touch,
Who will not keep you from their mirth
  Or tease you overmuch.
      " She will despise me ! " Be it so—
      But ask her why she let you go.

THE DREAM

You came to me in sleep last night,
  And stood beside my bed.
Your hands were white, your feet were white,
  But, oh, your cheeks were red!
" It is my guardian angel come
  To visit me," I said.

You stooped and kissed me on my face,
  Your lips were cold as stone,
And in its secret resting-place
  My heart made dolorous moan.
For you were there with me at last
  And still I was alone.

Nightlong I heard the passing-bell
  And knew the mourner's smart.
I heard a thousand churches knell
  The hour when we must part.
All night your icy kisses fell
  Upon my grieving heart.

THE DREAM

But, lo ! the blood of conquered shame
  Had filled your cheeks with red,
And roses molten out of flame
  Quickened the speechless dead,
Last night, when my belovèd came
  And kissed me in my bed.

TO RAIE

Boys in the sea may dive for silver pearls,
Or rob the spring of roses for their girls;
What pearls may deck, what roses can adorn
The princess of my morn?

A thousand seas have flung their treasure down
To kiss your feet, a thousand springs have thrown
Their ivory buds to make your bosom white
Too radiant for my sight.

And now you ask me for an earth-born song,
When all the dreams my eager senses long
To crown by day, cry from these nights of mine
For your lips' charmèd wine.

Kiss me and ease this passionate unrest,
There are so many voices in my breast
Singing, " Oh, eyes that shine ! Oh, lips that part !"
I cannot hear my heart.

TO RAIE

Kiss me and teach my voice ; my song shall take
New wings to heaven for your beauty's sake,
And by your lips inspired, will greet the birds
With new, triumphant words.

Lovers may dare the aching winter skies
For frosty stars to light their ladies' eyes ;
What star may deck, what planet can delight
The princess of my night ?

AFTER LOVE

LET there be lust between us two, my throat
    Is harsh with too much singing of faint songs,
My lips have numbered all the flowers by rote,
    But you to whom but one far rose belongs
May sing a better song than love's, and fill
My mouth with softer words than gardens thrill.

Perfume your lonely rose of youth, and crush
    My lips in ecstasy to stain it red,
And while we dream, the wanton night will hush
    Her errant birds, and close about our bed
Will hang her starry curtains cool with dew,
That your soft limbs may touch and glimmer through.

And I shall feel your passion of hot breath
    Strike on my lidded eyes, and fill my hair
With rumour of short nights, when summoned Death
    Came not to cool the scorched and withered air ;
But sleep betrayed her lover for a rhyme
That droned incessant on the lips of Time.

AFTER LOVE

And we shall sleep to-night, though not as they
  Who tread some strange, sweet story into dust,
And sing awhile, and lose the heart of day
  In child-like wanderings ; ours shall be lust
More fierce than life, than death more pitiless,
Our dawn shall be an utter weariness.

Yet, let them go, the loving and the glad,
  And hold me in your arms till I am chill ;
An autumn wonder made my childhood sad,
  But something of my childhood lingers still
And I am fain for toys. Take holiday
A little while from wondering, and play.

And I shall be the lover at your lips,
  Or now the thirsty babe that lies at morn
Upon your crownèd breasts, with what sweet sips
  It draws the honey forth. Ah ! to be born
So very wise in ignorance, and die
Unquiet for knowing nothing, you and I.

Or you shall lean upon my neck and speak
  Soft sorrows for my death, as you have missed
By one short hour the joy that lovers seek ;
  And dream your crimson mouth as yet unkissed,
Were crying for the moon, "God made me bold
Too late," while all Death left of me grew cold.

AFTER LOVE

There shall be pain between us two, and sound
  Of broken sword and ill-remembered song,
And we shall lead him captive, scourged and bound,
  The dear, blind boy who trembles for this wrong
Wrought at our hands. His tender face is wet,
Poor Love! But surely we shall not forget.

When the sad roses bow their heads to June,
  And lilies weep beneath the summer sky
For his sweet song, and all the world in tune
  Prays heaven for his mournful melody :
Our dream shall have an end, and we shall wake
The western hills with sorrow for his sake.

THE BLIND CRIPPLE

Lo! as I walked and nursed my bitter love
I saw a man who lay beside the street,
God for some sin had smitten off his feet
And wrought the blind, white face that drooped above
To such a shape of fear, that they who passed
Flung him scant alms aghast.

And horror lingered in the dusty air
And tumult of the street, though lovingly
From out the weary azure of the sky
The sunshine fell upon his fading hair,
The while beside the quivering, timid throng
His thin lips breathed a song.

And they have said that even as the blood
Of this blind cripple is the crimson wine
That greets the seasons in this heart of mine
And wakes my body with its passionate flood,
Calling, "Oh joy, my joy, thou art in vain,
The spring is come again!"

THE BLIND CRIPPLE

My love, my bitter love ! Ah God, that I
Were one with this poor, patient, suffering thing,
I should pay homage to my Lord the King,
And He would touch my eyelids tenderly,
Saying, " Poor eyes that were too brave to weep,
Yet knew no flower but sleep."

Ah God, that mine were such brave blood as this,
That leaps with life though his cropped limbs be stark,
And sets his pale lips singing in the dark,
For I have lost high heaven for a kiss,
And my poor spirit weeping to the wind
Is crippled, Lord, and blind.

And well I know that it is he who climbs
And he who sees, for me no wonder gleams
Upon the mountain-tops, as idle dreams
Are my fond memories and my poor rhymes ;
I can but fly and seek another place,
For envy of his grace.

TO THEM ALL

Oh, tearful maids and merry,
  With little mouths that take
Two bites to eat one cherry,
  How fine a world you make!
All joys and pains reproving
  That mar your pleasant strife—
When I am done with loving,
  May I be done with life!

I love you for your kisses,
  And yet I love withal
Those subtly teasing misses
  Who will not kiss at all.
I love you for your pleasure,
  I love you for your pain,
Your smiles are all my treasure,
  And your divine disdain.

Your little hands that tremble,
  In doing right—or wrong,
Your lips that can dissemble,
  But cannot hide your song,

TO THEM ALL

Your careless feet that wander
  Alike through earth and sky,
Are mine to win and squander
  And worship till I die.

Oh, laughing maids and weeping,
  With little hearts to take
Tired mortals from their sleeping
  And kiss the world awake,
The golden moments proving
  Mistress or queen or wife,
When I am done with loving,
  May I be done with life !

THE ARTIST

I AM only a dream that sings
    In a strange, large place,
And beats with impotent wings
    Against God's face.

The Darkness is all about,
    It hides the blue ;
But I conquer it with my shout,
    And pierce it through.

And the golden cities rise up
    Till I am as space,
And the earth is my drinking-cup
    And my resting-place.

And the stars that wonder above
    Cry out, " Oh, sweet !"
For mine are the wings of love
    And his silver feet.

THE ARTIST

And the stars that tremble below
    Are cold for fear,
For mine are his lips of snow
    And his scarlet tear.

But the sound of my shouting dies,
    And the shadows fall,
For Death is upon the skies
    And upon us all.

The shadows fall and the still,
    I am loath to sing,
I have wondered and kissed my fill
    On the lips of spring.

But the golden cities are gone
    And the stars are fled,
And I know that I am alone,
    And I am dead.

No more than a dream that sings
    In the streets of space ;
Ah, would that my soul had wings,
    Or a resting-place!

THE FAITHFUL POET

I'VE sung my song these many years
And kissed my lass, but, lo !
My lips grow weary now ;
My eyes are fonder far of tears
Than seeing girls' glad faces ; pain
Is mistress of my heart again.

Still these too mournful moments prove
No penitence, for lo !
Dear heart, I do not know
That there is anything but love
To tune a song or make amends
For our sad lives and tuneless ends.

REGRET

SILVER rose was the morning, his breast was strewn
    with pearls—
Spoil of the dew-bright cherry that danced along the
    spray,
And I saw the sun of beauty shine out in the eyes
    of girls
Who bowed their limbs to the morning, for love
    of the primrose way.

The splendour of waking beauty had filled my world
    with joy,
Red for the roses and green for the hills whence the
    skies depart,
A secret song for the maiden, a silver pipe for the boy,
To echo and bring her blithely, to his arms, to his
    lips, to his heart.

Ah ! to dream and awake—to have seen and to see
    no more !
The roses falter and perish, the clouds droop low
    on the hill,
And the secret song of the maiden that was so
    sweet before
Is still with the pipe of the boy, as my echoing
    heart is still.

REGRET

They come not the shining hours, with their trea-
    sure of green and of gold,
Trooping across the meadows, as they came once
    on a day ;
Mine the monotonous years and the sorrow of
    growing old,
Mine to weep for the morning, far down on the
    primrose way.

DOROTHY

SHE stole across the wood by night,
  The branches swayed to let her pass,
Dorothy in the moonlight
  Treading the dewy grass.

And so she came to the quiet pool
  In whose enchanted deep
The white moon makes her body cool
  And tired stars lie asleep.

She loosed her girdle's golden link,
  Her soft robes touched her feet,
And wakeful birds that came to drink
  Fell dumb—she was so sweet.

She saw her image dreaming there,
  More glad and calm than she,
And a great comfort filled the air
  And the soul of Dorothy.

For mirrored in the shining well
  The wind might hardly stir—
Her ivory body rose and fell,
  Her sad lips smiled at her.

DOROTHY

Ah, happier than the starry night,
  And gladder than the day,
Dorothy in the moonlight
  Threw the world away !

And in the pool she lay at rest,
  Quiet and deathly fair ;
The gentle waves her throat caressed,
  And combed her golden hair.

Her eyes saw other stars than those
  That wondered in the sky ;
Her heart had found another rose
  Than love's, that would not die.

The moonlight was her shroud, she lay
  Upon a regal bed—
The Queen who flung the world away,
  Who died and is not dead.

For ever in my dreams by night
  I wait to see her pass—
Dorothy in the moonlight
  Treading the dewy grass.

THE NEW DAWN

TAKE all my dreams, yes, take them all,
The splendid fabric of my play,
Flowers of the starry carnival,
But spare my little hour of day.
Leave me my lilies tall and white
That tremble in the morning's dew ;
I need no blossoms of the night,
No moonlit buds for my delight
Or sombre groves of yew.

I wandered many and many a time
Where sleep-lit lanterns threw their beams,
And gathered blooms of scented rhyme
To fashion garlands for my dreams.
Why seek, I thought, a wakeful flower,
When these I hold are fairer far,
That thrill across the midnight hour
The shadows of Titania's bower,
And praise the evening star.

But then she came, and lo ! it seemed
I had forgotten life too long—
God had perfected while I dreamed
Another world, another song.

THE NEW DAWN

'Twas not to ask in what shy mood
The white day found her standing there,
I, who had never understood
What might be bad—what might be good:
I knew that she was fair.

I think God meant my eyes to see
How fair she was, I think my voice
Was made to praise the harmony
Of this His labour, and rejoice.
And well I know these tears of mine
Because she lies not on my heart,
More than His roses red with wine,
More than His myriad stars that shine,
Acclaim His perfect art.

For all the rich and curious things
That I have found within my sleep,
Are nought beside this child that sings
Among the heather and the sheep;
And I, who with expectant eyes
Have fared across the star-lit foam,
See through my dreams a new sun rise
To conquer unachievèd skies,
And bring the dreamer home.

TO E. M. D.

AFTER love's bitter words be mine the skies
  And tranquil fields of this dream-haunted place,
The gentle welcome of your sad, sweet eyes,
  The kindness and the pity of your face :
My little sister ! be it mine to see,
  In these remote and disillusioned hours,
  You in your garden of imagined flowers
Dreaming your tender dreams to comfort me.

Not in these glades should luckless lovers weep
  Or mourn their passion in these meadows dim :
Shaped like a flower new-moulded out of sleep
  I see your body, marvellously slim,
Gleam in the dusk, I hear the murmurous song
  Of drowsy childhood charm the listening night,
  And with an all-dispassionate delight
My heart takes rest, that love has claimed too long.

Ah child so kind to me ! I have been far
  Across the world that never was my own
Seeking a cruel and resentful star ;
  But now in calmer hours than I have known,

TO E. M. D.

Your spirit leads me on through moor and hill
    To these quiet fields where dreamy children play ;
    Keep me from loving, blessèd child, and stay
Within my heart, my little sister still !

TO TIME

Time ! you old dotard prosing endlessly
To bore a graceless world, and leave our sky
Sadder than rain or any wise man's tears,
I crave no part in your monotony,
But ask one favour, being born to die,
Grant me my moments, you may keep your years.

THE DREAMER WAKES

IF all the world's my dream,
Why do I dream so ill?
These stars that do not gleam,
This wind, forlorn and chill,
That discontents the years,
Shall not allay my tears.

Then dream, my heart, no more—
Let that dim Power who made
Our primal dust restore
His plan, and unafraid
We'll spread our sightless wings
Into the truth of things.

They will not hurt so much
As this vain dream of mine,
This feast no man may touch,
This draught of bitter wine;
Be wakeful then, oh heart,
And bid the dream depart.

THE DREAMER WAKES

Under the morning star
I shall arise and know
Who led my steps so far
And set me dreaming so,
And to life's chorus then
My lips shall cry Amen!

THE DREAM THAT HAS NO END

THE winter trails its weary hours,
 The night begins ere day is over,
But mine are all the summer flowers,
 I am that prince of fools, a lover.
Yet passion will not so inspire
 My days that I may heap my treasure;
Slave of an incomplete desire,
 I won my dream and took my pleasure.

Life has found many flowers to fill
 My heart, too eager to disdain them;
I kissed my girl and did not kill,
 I held her hands and did not stain them.
And that is why she haunts me now
 In sombre hours God made for sleeping,
With her serene, indifferent brow,
 And her soft eyes for ever weeping.

Ah, God, that I as other men
 Might love, and love no more; to sever
A fragrant blossom now and then,
 To kiss and be at peace for ever!

THE DREAM THAT HAS NO END

But I am faithful in this wise
   That having found I still must keep her,
   With her cold heart and tender eyes,
Till dawn brings solace to the sleeper.

THE BOY-WORLD

THIS is a young world
  With blossoms in his hair,
The green grass newly curled
  That squanders everywhere ;
He was born yesterday,
  He is too young for sorrow,
He sings the hours away
  With ballads of to-morrow.

Only a little lad
  With nothing to forget,
Knowing nor good nor bad
  Who has not found them yet ;
We must not blame him, no !
  Wisdom will follow after,
The things that hurt us so
  Are hidden from his laughter.

Lord of the spring-tide joys
  Unknown of doubt or shame ;
We are the careless toys
  That help him in his game.

THE BOY-WORLD

He bends us to his will,
  Our prayers are checked half-spoken,
Youth will be master still
  Though all his toys are broken.

He sings his song and plays—
  How might he understand
We count the weary days
  Beneath his eager hand ?
He laughs above his sport,
  We tremble at the thunder,
And all our plans are nought
  Who only wait and wonder.

Yet this is ours, to trace
  Through field and copse and hill,
The beauty of his face
  That smiles upon us still ;
So fair he is and young
  His joy is ours to cherish,
Though all our songs are sung
  And all the singers perish.

SERENADE

By day my timid passions stand
　Like begging children at your gate,
Each with a mute, appealing hand
　To ask a dole of Fate;
But when night comes, released from doubt,
　Like merry minstrels they appear,
The stars ring out their hopeful shout,
　Belovèd, can you hear?

They dare not sing to you by day
　Their all-desirous song, or take
The world with their adventurous lay
　For your enchanted sake.
But when the night-wind wakes and thrills
　The shadows that the night unbars,
Their music fills the dreamy hills,
　And folds the friendly stars.

Belovèd, can you hear? They sing
　Words that no mortal lips can sound;
Love through the world has taken wing,
　My passions are unbound.

SERENADE

And now, and now, my lips, my eyes,
    Are stricken dumb with hope and fear,
It is my burning soul that cries,
    Belovèd, can you hear?

THE BUTTERFLY

Along the lane as I passed by
I saw a sulphur butterfly
Fanning with newly powdered wing
The laughing breezes of the Spring;
From brown to green, from green to blue
Lightly the fond adventurer flew,
And so, I thought, if she were here,
Christine would charm the waking year.

Ah, heart! that all unwilling stirs
To greet the song that is not hers—
The song my quick, unfaithful blood
Sings for the breaking of the bud
And earth made young again, shall you
Whom all the Winter-time held true
Change for a yellow bribe and wait
To praise the traitor at his gate?

The flowers of Spring, his azure skies,
Are not more lovely than her eyes,
Glad with unfathomable dreams;
The music of his winds, his streams,
With her soft lips may not compete
That grant the echoes silver feet
To foot it on the hills; the Spring
Hath no such songs as she can sing.

THE BUTTERFLY

I may not hear her in this place,—
Or watch the ripples in her face
Where glad emotions play, or find
The loveliness that makes me blind.
Not in the happy fields that know
The beating of her heart I go,
Nor where her careless, little feet,
Tread on the earth and make it sweet.

The pageant of the Summer comes,
With waving flags and joyful drums,
With pomp of leaf and pride of flower,
And many a green and cheerful hour.
Under the wide and shining arch
I see the blue procession march,
And on the wind of Spring is borne
The perfume of a Summer morn.

The Summer comes and Winter dies,
And now the new-born butterflies
Proclaim the Spring—I saw one pass
A primrose blossom through the grass.
But, heart, the joyous insect brings
No message on its powdered wings
For you and me, who yet must stay
Far from our love this Winter day.

CHRISTINE REVISITED

WITHIN the garden of my heart once more
  She walks, and wakes the echoes of my heart
With her glad lips grown kinder than before.
  Welcome, belovèd ! never more depart.
    My eyes have wearied for you, and my days
    Have seemed but sorrow, lacking your sweet ways.

Nay, though I be a captive for all time—
  Heap, love, your chains upon me, bind me close
With your fierce fetters—still my happy rhyme
  Shall sound the praise of the eternal rose
    That shares my prison, and within my bars
    God shall bring forth a thousand singing stars.

I have been free, and had all heaven and hell
  For prison, until my piteous hands grew sore
Striking the voiceless walls : now it is well
  Even though I be a captive evermore.
    My grateful song shall fill my hiding-place
    To find Eternity hath so sweet a face.

NOCTURNE

WHEN Sleep puts on the cloak of Death,
   And in the city masquerades,
Earth's tired children fight for breath,
   And they who sought the dreamy glades
     Fall panting on the road, and lie
     Like clods beneath the sombre sky.

But when Death comes like gentle sleep,
   And takes our children to his breast,
Our weary eyes forbear to weep—
   It is so very good to rest
     Quietly in the dreamy corn
     Until the breaking of the morn.

TO MÉLISANDE

Now is the morning very fair,
  On every leaf the dew is lit,
Oh heart of mine, let down your hair
  And all the winds shall play with it.

Across my face, across mine eyes
  The winds shall blow for my delight
The curtain of your hair, the skies
  Shall win the pomp of night.

And all about my head shall wreathe
  New winds and blossoms new,
And yours shall be the air I breathe
  And all my darkness, you.

The tears the sunlit roses weep
  May not assuage my pain,
Mine are the broken stars of sleep
  And the cool night again.

Within the shadow of our dreams
  I draw my little breath
And I heed not the sunbeams,
  I have no care for death.

TO MÉLISANDE

Nay, though the mocker everywhere
  Echoes his jest and stales his wit,
Let down your hair, let down your hair,
  I'll make my shroud of it.

"IN FORMA PAUPERIS"

I HAVE no silks or satins fine
  With broidered flowers for her to wear,
I have no diamonds to shine
  Among the shadows of her hair;
But when we meet, in every tress
  I see a jewelled tear-drop gleam,
And she is robed like a princess
  All in the fabric of my dream.

I have no sunny garden-close
  Where we may hear the summer call,
Never a lily, never a rose,
  To grace the sweetest flower of all;
But gladder seasons, rarer flowers,
  Blow in the starlight cool and deep,
And we can pluck the fragrant hours
  Within our pleasant land of sleep.

I may not see her when I will
  To pledge my love and win her smile,
And yet we are together still,
  And we are happy all the while;

"IN FORMA PAUPERIS"

For well we know that God will give
  To two poor lovers yet a day
To live the hours they did not live,
  And say the things they did not say.

ONE MORE SONG

AWAKE oh heart! oh passionate lips conspire
  To sound a new glad poem for my love,
So may she know the whole of the desire
    That fills my veins, these bruisèd words may prove
      How all night long I burn and grieve and pray,
      And how I seek her all the lifelong day.

For I am lost in her sweet ways where grow
  Roses and lilies to enchant the dead,
There is no part of me that does not know
    How her curls tremble, how her small feet tread
      Blessing the earth, and how her fingers play
      Like gentle children with the winds of day.

And when I touch her glowing arm I feel
  The little veins beneath her silken skin
Playing, and through my thirsty flesh there steal
    The rivers of her blood that leap within ;
      It is her blood that fires the words I speak,
      And mine that fills the blushes of her cheek.

ONE MORE SONG

And when in dreams my lips repose on hers
  Kissing the pretty words that nestle there,
Her sweetness numbs my aching brain and stirs
    Like a dim sound of her, the dream-hushed air,
      And through the gates of sleep I hear her call
      My drowsy senses to the carnival.

Love, that surpassing all my dreams of love
  Is yet so dearly mine, my fate defies,
I care not in what sombre world I move
  Seeing the universe with her soft eyes,
    With her brave feet to bear me in the dance
    Forgotten is my poor inheritance.

This crumbling house, my body, is made new
  Now by the very fire and fret of love
That has transfused its chambers and pierced through
  Its dusty casements till the stars above
    Smile in upon me, and the winds that start
    Laughing from Heaven beat upon my heart.

And as a bud is shaken into flower
  By spring's last wind to dream no more alone,
Serving the pomp of summer, so love's power
  Has overtaken me, and I am one
    In that far world of love mine eyes have seen
    With all the lovers that have ever been.

ONE MORE SONG

Ours is one eloquence and ours one song,
  And we are noted by our shining eyes
And restless hands ; we wander all life long
    In worlds unearthly, now with tender sighs
      Wooing the hills of passion, now with tears
      Mourning the grim procession of the years.

Yet ever do we pray that we may keep
  Our love immaculate although we die
Being our all ; the clouds her teardrops weep,
    Her laughter fills the sunshine, earth and sky
      Are but as shades of her, and we who sing
      The lutes she plays upon to call the spring.

Oh my belovèd ! How shall I tell in words
  The pride of all love's lovers, men have writ
Passing the song of children and of birds,
    To ease their hearts, and have not compassed it ;
      How shall I murmur with the tranquil dove,
      When I am deaf and blind and dumb with love !

In desert nights and leafy forest days
  I have discovered you, and where the lips
Of drownèd sailors sing faint roundelays
    Along the decks of overwhelmèd ships
      Your name is sung, and echoing overhead
      The sea-birds cry it to the patient dead.

ONE MORE SONG

The nightingale across the crimson bowl
  Gave you to Omar ; by the forsaken waves
Ulysses found you dreaming ; Shakespeare's soul
  Drew its clear song from yours ; and sullen slaves
    Peered on your beauty through their heavy lids
    And with their hearts' blood built the Pyramids.

There is no time in love, nor death nor birth,
  Star whispers unto star, the white buds flower
In crimson ecstasy, and on the earth
  The lovers capture their eternal hour ;
    We were, we are, we shall be ; land and sea
    Change, but our love endureth endlessly.

DRINKING SONG FOR LOVERS

When all the summer airs fall still
  Hushed by the stars that shine,
High in the tavern on the hill
  The topers quaff their wine ;
Their merry song takes eager wing
  Across the silent town,
And echo breathes the words they sing
  As I go dreaming down.

Have I no wine, who linger yet
  In vineyards cool and far,
Where every vine is dewy wet
  And every grape a star ?
Where tranquil hours like bubbles rise
  To glitter and depart,
Where I am master of her eyes
  And servant of her heart ?

Not mine to see the daylight slink,
  A fuddled toper, in ;
It is the wine of love I drink
  From an enchanted bin ;

DRINKING SONG FOR LOVERS

And it is mine to offer up
  Praise to the gods above,
That I may drain their loving-cup
  Till I am drunk with love.

Day blossoms in the world below,
  And with reluctant feet
I hear the weary bibbers go
  Along the shameful street ;
With merry voice and flitting wings
  The birds acclaim the east,
But still the magic vintner brings
  New flagons to the feast.

Ah, crimson lip and ivory breast !
  From what tremendous vine
Was this immortal vintage pressed,
  This never-quenching wine ?
What sunshine kissed it, what warm rains
  Swelled the smooth grapes, and made
This godlike draught to fire my veins
  And keep me undismayed !

May I drink deep of love and long
  Until the morning cries
The burden of my drinking-song,
  The wonder of her eyes ;

DRINKING SONG FOR LOVERS

Till, lulled by the bewitchèd bowl,
  My passions fall asleep.
Deeper and yet more deep, my soul,
  O heart of mine, drink deep!

THE LAST SERENADE

COURAGE, my song, and like a lover climb
  To her high balcony; this is the night
When in a star-lit valley where old Time
  Pauses to latch his way-worn shoe, delight
Shall blossom like a flower; though she rest
  Within her highest turret, this my song
Shall bring her down to my insurgent breast
  Where the blood burns that has been cool too long.

Be silent now, oh, moon, and be you dumb,
  Oh too importunate stars! I will not hear
Your dulcet tales that make my senses numb
  With easeless longing, for the hour is near
When I will go, who with my love abide,
  Dreaming across your luminous seas no more
To the far gates of heaven, where the tide
  Flings wrack of worlds upon the reverberate shore.

Nay, though my eyes grieve for the way we went,
  Peace shall attend my heart and love shall steep
My passionate soul in waters of content;
  No more enamoured of my lady Sleep

133

THE LAST SERENADE

I shall explore in tranquil wakefulness
   My love's own universe ; her little hands,
Her eyes, her lips, are all my loveliness,
   And these are all my heritable lands.

This is the end of all things, thou shalt cease,
   Oh heart, thy timeless journey followed far,
For all thy days shall be inviolate peace
   And all thy starry nights shall know one star
Irradiant and serene ; and thou, oh mind,
   Weary of thy long questionings, shalt prove
Servant of my enchanted life and find
   In all thy ways the wisdom that is love.

The world is drunk with night, there gather slow
   From some remoter heaven to tempt my blood
The mutable stars processional, and lo !
   On all the hills the moonlight is in flood ;
But I am wakeful yet. Oh song, ascend
   Swift to her ears and bid her dreams depart.
To-night the sombre years shall have an end,
   To-night, to-night shall bring her to my heart !

THE LASS THAT DIED OF LOVE

LIFE is not dear or gay
  Till lovers kiss it,
Love stole my life away
  Ere I might miss it.
In sober March I vowed
  I'd have no lover,
Love laid me in my shroud
  Ere June was over.

I felt his body take
  My body to it,
And knew my heart would break
  Ere I should rue it ;
June roses are not sad
  When dew-drops steep them,
My moments were so glad
  I could not keep them.

Proud was I love had made
  Desire to fill me,
I shut my eyes and prayed
  That he might kill me.

THE LASS THAT DIED OF LOVE

I saw new wonders wreathe
   The stars above him,
And oh, I could not breathe
   For kissing of him.

Is love too sweet to last,
   Too fierce to cherish,
Can kisses fall too fast
   And lovers perish?
Who heeds since love disarms
   Death, ere we near him,
Within my lover's arms
   I did not fear him!

But since I died in sin
   And all unshriven,
They would not let me win
   Into their heaven;
They would not let my bier
   Into God's garden,
But bade me tarry here
   And pray for pardon.

I lie and wait for grace
   That shall surround me,
His kisses on my face,
   His arms around me;

THE LASS THAT DIED OF LOVE

> And sinless maids draw near
>   To drop above me,
> A virginal sad tear
>   For envy of me.

THE ASCETIC'S LOVE-SONG

In a long valley of the wakeful night
  I found her first who leaves me nevermore,
She only being constant, in my sight
    Many have stood and made mine eyelids sore
      With sorrow of brief loving, as the tides
      Triumph the dream of love, but Pain abides.

She doth not call me old ; in her embrace
  My body is made lovely, intricate
With throbbing veins and nerves that interlace
    My bones with threads of fire ; more passionate
      Then any mortal love, she stirs in me
      Splendour of life beyond mortality.

For at her kiss my senses wake, mine eyes
  Win braver colours than our sunsets hold,
My ears achieve the deathless melodies
    Our songs but faintly echo, I behold
      My soul, a timid human thing, a-nod
      In the vast body of a tortured god.

THE ASCETIC'S LOVE-SONG

And my ambitious earth that would not rest
  Cold in the grave, but sought imperfect form
Climbs to divinity upon her breast
  And takes the kingdom of the gods by storm;
    I am beloved of Pain, and she doth make
    My flesh immortal for her welcome's sake.

Cleansing the mortal part of me with fire
  Of her consuming love, I am made pure;
I am the singing child of her desire,
  The blossom of her passion, I endure
    A million lives, yet ever by my side
    There stays the burning body of my bride.

And this is life indeed, by sleep forsworn
  I feel the anguish of my rotting clay
That yearned for godhead, dying to be born
  A thousand times to die, and night and day
    I droop with life's excess,' who once would
      plan
    That at the last I might be more than man.

But serving her, our souls seem nothing worth,
  Fashioned by idle apes for apes to wear;
There's never a weeping thing upon the earth
  That knows itself immortal, but we dare
    To make our frail humanity our pride,
    And by our senses we are crucified.

THE ASCETIC'S LOVE-SONG

Her love exalted us like new-pressed wine,
  Nightlong I see great limbs that writhe and
    sprawl
Upon a shrunken world, and they are mine.
  I taste the torment of the buds that fall
    Spoil of the frantic seasons, and forlorn
    I share the anguish of the pregnant corn.

And o'er my aching consciousness there sways
  The poised image of incarnate pain,
With ruddy hair and cheek and eyes that blaze
  Despotic in desire, I bid her reign'
    Empress of my aspiring dust, and kill
    My rebel soul that would be master still.

For love is sorrow's sublimate, and tears
  Are the last words of lovers, there survives
After the brilliant frenzy of our years,
  Our memory of these ; our little lives
    Make but a sorry tale, until we go
    Invulnerable with remembered woe.

Once, when the pallid shadows of the day
  Achieved the shape of woman, I was fain
To prove my manhood, now I take my way
  Wearing the token of my mistress Pain,
    For she is constant, round me she doth fold
    Closer her arms, though I am passing old.

TO AN IDLE POET

Ah, poet! dreaming still? The future weaves
New threads of silver for your careless head.
In vain the arrow of your years is sped
To reach the goal you wot not : now it cleaves
The airs of sleep where drowsy wonder grieves
Fast in the grave of the forgotten dead.
Lo ! all your gallant words are yet unsaid,
And all your songs but silence. Time deceives
Your little hour with gift of greener leaves
And fairer flowers ; and, dreaming in your bed
The dream eternal, you shall soon be shed
As poppy-stalks among the gladdening sheaves,
As dust among the corn unwinnowèd.

Ah, poet! dreaming still, who should but weep
For sorrow of the moments falling fast,
And years of wonder perished while you passed
Treading the very gentle ways of sleep
Because the mountains of the world are steep :
Why leapt your blood to life, that now at last
You should take refuge in your dream, aghast
Before the glory of the heavenly deep
Where frail ships strive to God with pitiful mast ?

TO AN IDLE POET

Arise and make the world your own! Though now
  The better years are gone, there linger still
  Glad memories where dawn on field and hill
Trod while you slept. Towards the mountain's brow
Night gently leads her peace. Awake and vow
  All to the world! Before the shadows kill
  Shake off the chains of sleep : the merest rill
Shall heed your word, the tallest tree shall bow,
  And you shall make the mountains what you will.

For though man only lives his sombre days
  To sicken at his task of life and die,
  Dreading the silent and unfriendly sky
That has not heard his message, still he plays
His part in God's great pageant, and obeys
  His soul's command, albeit grudgingly;
  And where his hesitant feet have wandered by,
His footprints scar the world, and by his ways
A hundred ages tread ; his heedless phrase
  Rings in their ears like an angelic cry
  Heard before birth and treasured timelessly,
And all his timid hopes and quick dismays
  Thrill in their hearts and build their heaven on high.

And though your joyful tales be left half told,
  Your songs but tuneful moments that might be,
  Your children's children at their mother's knee
Shall whisper them and shall not find them old,

TO AN IDLE POET

Saying "Our fathers were of sterner mould
  Who tore grim secrets from the cruel sea
  That beats upon our hearts." Your words, set
    free
From taint of mortal lip, shall make them bold
To dare the great adventure, and behold
  Truth as a goddess throned eternally
  Upon the lives of men. You hold the key
To all the future and its brighter gold,
  And unborn ages wait on your decree.

Then, poet, dream no more! Creative spring
  Bends to her task, and summer's at the gate
  Calling the scarlet poppies. Soon or late
Autumn will scattter them unpitying
Before the coming of the frosty king.
  So shall it be with your imagined state,
  Your visionary pomp : Time shall abate
The hoarded treasure of your dreams and bring
The dreamer to the dust on shattered wing.
  Your children shall not know you, love and hate
  And fear shall pass you by, and you shall wait
As one who has not lived, for Death to sing
  Your weakness and your sorrow and your fate.

ENVOI

ALL the drear summer time in hot and dusty places
  We watched the roses die, and still our lips
  Made black by thirst, sang bravely of the ships
That brought us to the isle of lovely faces,
While yet our youth held all the world in fee,
And dared the stars from an exultant sea.

No more in haunts of green the maidens bound
    their posies,
  No more their laughter leapt to greet the May,
  There was an end of our brief holiday,
And there was no more passion in our roses ;
So one by one we watched the petals fall,
And found no buds to grace the carnival.

And yet of nights, we sang, long nights and tired
    morrows,
  And yet we sang of our delicious spring.
  The magnificent ruling-time of love, our King,
Whose name made sweet our lips within our
    sorrows ;
And thus we built fair dreams of delicate rhyme,
Far from our palaces, all the long summer time.